Of Our Elaborate Plans…

Also by Fred Rosenblum

Hollow Tin Jingles (Main Street Rag 2014)

Vietnumb (Fomite Press 2018)

Playing Chicken with an Iron Horse (Fomite Press 2019)

Tramping Solo (Fomite Press 2021)

Our Gray City's Face to the Frozen Sea (Cholla Needles 2023)

Of Our Elaborate Plans...

Fred Rosenblum

Fomite
Burlington VT

ISBN-13: 978-1-959984-55-9
Library of Congress Control Number: 2024935024

Fomite
58 Peru Street
Burlington, VT 05401

09/23/2024

for Andy

Some of the following were initially published by *the Aurorean,*
Cholla Needles, The Courtship of Winds, Harbinger Asylum, Pudding
Magazine, and San Diego Reader

Contents

Foreword

My first exposure to Fred Rosenblum's poetry was in a San Diego writers' workshop where I, new to the group, was crowd-testing scenes from my play-in-progress and Fred was working on a poem. Fred had read only a few stanzas of the piece when I was gripped by the mounting, staggering power of the poem: a hallucinogenic howl from his tour as a young U. S. Marine in Southeast Asia during, as the Vietnamese called it, "The American War." I knew I was in the presence of artistic greatness. Tears welled in my eyes, as much from my gut-level response to the poet's *cri de coeur* as from my unbidden flashback to a day in downtown Chicago in 1965 when a U. S. Army corporal told me I was medically exempt from the military draft.

On our second walk together, as Fred and I were becoming — in Kerouac's peerless phrase — "heartbreaking new friends," I found myself recounting for him the complete history of my first marriage and its demise, including details known to only a select few of my most intimate, longtime, acquaintances. As we approached the café which was our destination, I said, "Shit, Fred, I haven't talked so openly about this to anyone since I can't remember when. But it's impossible to hold back with you, because you are, literally, an open book."

And so he is: a literal open book — as you soon realize when you read any one of Fred's poems in this magnificent collection: *Of Our Elaborate Plans*; indeed across his entire body of work. You see, over the course of his long writing career, Rosenblum has crafted a unique style of candidly autobiographical, hybridized poetry/prose. Yes, he cites Bukowski in this collection, even suggesting a poetic kinship with Bukowski's hard-drinking mail carrier literary alter ego Henry Chinaski; and Fred's readers may also glean the influence of the Beats across all of his work. You will recognize, too, a reference to Jim Morrison's "The End", as sourced by the title of this collection.

But in *Of Our Elaborate Plans*, his 6th collection, Fred's style is singular and mature — Rosenblumian, I suggest. One delights in his agile, assured, prose/poetry meld. And here's the thing: as the cumulative power of Fred's words and imagery wash over you, you find yourself helpless, free-diving deep into your own storied biography and discovering sunken treasures down there in your own fecund mud, as happened to me in that San Diego workshop. Such is the seductive power of Fred Rosenblum's art.

And seductive, indeed, are the poems in *Of Our Elaborate Plans*. With the first 17 syllables of the collection — in "Haiku Sunflower" — the poet delivers such delightful imagery, with a Rosenblumian touch of humor, that your guarded heart leaps; you remember that old photo of your mother, perhaps, smiling in that eternal field of teetering sunflowers.

But the majesty of this collection lies in its awesome, awful, inevitability: its promise of 'The End' fulfilled.

You'll find the poet early in the collection delighting in Nature, zealously digging in the earth; digging up the stars and the moon and the sun; digging up people of the earth, even his "bumpkin" self; unearthing trees and streams, wind and rain and maggots; making extravagant plans to cultivate a garden, to test his mettle, to ogle a nice ass, to love, to make and raise children. To have a life. Just like you and me.

But as the collection grows dark, gothic, twenty Arcadian acres are traded for 1200 square feet high up in an urban tower — wind-blown newspapers swirling amongst the unhoused on the gritty concrete at its feet; Nature's elaborate plans sputter to a spitting rain on an anemic dawn, and the poet finds himself "rife with lipomas," "scheduled for procedures," wearing elastic-waistband trousers, and unable to hear for shit, just like you and me . . . Like most of Fred Rosenblum's collections, *Of Our Elaborate Plans* is a roughly chronological grand arc of autobiographical story, moving fearlessly through beginning, middle and end. But unique to this collection, is an urgent meditation on The End. The Ultimate.

So, dear Reader, I encourage you to read on! Experience the evocative power of this collection. And if you, like me, begin to question why you yourself plan so elaborately — why you scheme, plot and contrive so ferociously — just to end up "a mile or so from oblivion," you might anticipate the poet's words and shout out from your heart of hearts—

… most of us want to
realize something large before we are
a figment to the rotten fruit in these
annals of arbitrary human life
on Earth!

—William Damkoehler
Actor, director, playwright, educator

Washington State

Haiku Sunflower

Blackcaps ride the face
Of a giant on the wind
Its feeder teeters

"There are very few professions in which people just sit down and think hard for five or six hours a day all by themselves. Of course it's why you want to become a writer — because you have the liberty to do that, but once you have the liberty you also have the obligation to do it."
—Tobias Wolff

Tobias Wolff Country

I woke to the smell of Wild Turkey in my beard.
Sunlight beating on the walls ...
Wake up Bukowski ! Chinaski! Rosenblum!
said the hungover sun to the douchebag
bum. County outside choking on the early
morning vapors of human waste — get up
and smell the manure! So I drank a warm
beer & climbed through the window of my
broken truck door, drove the fifty miles of
SR. 9 farmland — smoked a number and
sorted the mail. Time to pay my union dues.
Hit the street. Park and loop. I'd refuse
to deliver an irascible asshat
of a laid-off logger's entitlement check
...'cuz his snarlin', ain't no darlin' of a dawg,
petitioned its hirsute gawd
with a prayer and then beseeched me
on his dilapidated cedar porch —
Sedro Wooley Dawg: ... *that you dare not trod*
the mossy breadth of my front yard sod,
saunter to my master's mail receptacle,
remiss in your approach, an admonition
garbled in a slurry of fang-baring drool.
And after wiping the fur and that slobber
from my steel-toed boot, I tripped
on the slick-with-drizzle
prolapse of hazelnut roots;

stomped through the flowering tulips
just nigh of noon, when blackberries
and bologna sandwiches awaited me,
and my ravenous pangs for devouring
near the castor-gnawed and teetering timbers,
where a murder cawed in a stand of hemlock
… bounced like embers
atop the heaps of Karmann Ghias
rusting in the steady rain and where
three generations of quasi-toothless,
tobacky-chewin' tar heels,
ran a salvage yard off the North Cascade Hwy.
All those years of the wet scrap rescued,
secreted an odor of fresh-cut liver
where logging trucks bolted by
as lightning before thunder,
and drowned-out the cold angry gargle
from the throat of the Skagit River.

The Morning Paper (or poet likens POTUS to penis)

I stop to water
an umbrella of licorice fern,
offering moist asylum
to a banana slug
who feasts on microbes
and is content in the slime
of its nature.
I stop to release
amid my groggy morning stumble
to retrieve the newspaper
containing a curiously
inappropriate political cartoon —
a satire depicting
what would earn the ire
of our tidy bucolic community
beholden to the virtues
of Christians and Christianity.
I put the POTUS
back into my pants
and piss down my leg
— not an irreverent gesture
but a mere circumstance
of incontinence, I can assure you.

Horseplay

Have you heard of this horse prank
played in the sundown's
settling soups of fog
on farmers scattering
hanks of timothy and alfalfa hay?
Uncanny how,
we'd report, in synchrony
and in precise, fabulous detail,
the storied, two-headed, *trompe l'oeil*
— an anomaly, and/or freak of nature,
as I had, with my own eyes seen.
Imagine the sniggering of the whinnies
and the neighs. I wish I'd recorded
or taken a picture of sorts
out amid that inaudible mist
and the unsettling of snorts,
opposing, juxtaposing,
front side, backside, head to tail
— tail to head. A luster slightly shy of sepia
resting on the dusky bare backs
of the oft-time laboring teams
out where, in autumn's early
evening meadow, a playful jape meant to deceive
 a country bumpkin … namely me.

The Day before the Day I Cut My Thumb at the Pump House

I cinched-up some of the ill-fitting
leftover canvas tatters
from my timbering and tobacco days,
when Copenhagen
took a gradual divot from my gum line
...headed-out to an acre where I
defined myself with rake,
loppers, and spade,
toted some dahlia tubers and tulip bulbs,
old standby elixirs for what ailed me,
a perennial *ennui* — existential plague
— prodded me with a compulsion
to claw into last season's
composted, cow manure sod,
where I'd hurled some of the hirsute,
hayseed clods, flecked with evidence of clay,
at rascal, brush tail gray squirrels rivaling,
insolent, squalling
... blue-black Mohawk, Stellar Jays
both, inherently heavy into the hazelnuts
as I grimaced with my necessity
to crouch at the bedsides
of our garlic's shriveling tentacles
that I'd set aside to dry.

My lumbago in the tomato house
primed me with the realization
that this garden,
with its three-dimensional limestone pools,
before a fir and an alder curtain,
in all probability, held within it
the myriad pastoral props for collaborating
on elevating one's sense of being.

And as the wane of day arrived on these
already-expired eyelids laden
with a spate of late morning trips
to the refrigerator brewery
and where heavy too
a cottonwood rheum
personified the groggy isolation
on dusk's field blushing.
Its feeble streaks of light,
half-faced on a rusted shovel stabbing
the cool earth rich with the wormy castings
of subterranean biding.

Sun Polishes Moon

Autumn's dying ember sinks,
quenches way out there
where it meets the sea.
Heavenly bodies
patiently await
the inevitable darkness
as tides recede
and supple boughs
dance on bellows brisk.
Then astral gems begin to sparkle,
start to come alive ... exist
on the obsidian backs of algae
and plankton diners,
crustaceans indecisively appearing
to dither beneath curtains of hemlock,
alder, and our golden orb of night,
where the natural satellite
waxes in the wake of a murder
climbing the cold, clear sky,
traversing the smirk on the face
& across its illusory eyes.
Caws fade with distance
as I breathe deep this evening's ocean air.

On Patrol

A robin skews its head,
watches for a wriggle
in the mossy sponge
of the spring earth.

A resident rabbit
squats on quilted haunches,
gnaws an entry
into the orchard fence,
possibly a bit bemused by the obvious,
bird with bird,
yet has no real interest or aspirations
in slinky delights.

Flies buzz by and bound
on the magnifying glass
of the midday prelude
to summer's sun-bleached,
cordwood leeching
at the edge of the forest
teeming with game trails
legible in the dry stucco
impressions of seasonal mud.

The eyes of a black tail
engage me amid the puzzling
mosaic of pruned magenta
dogwood shoots. Its fawn,
where breezy willow saplings arc
conceals itself in the luxuriant,
stained-glass windows of wood,
gives me a bit of a start;
its ruminant angst intrinsic,

albeit, these animals are used to me
and my frequent patrols.
While I continue my surveillance
their foraging stares remain vigilant,
though I've done nothing
to alarm them.

Yesterday, this same fawn —
same for its distinction in the dawn,
trembling with a morning chill ...
around thirty-five degrees,
before the tower near the rill,
gave me another start
on a trail marked
by the turquoise litter of eggshell shards.
A spasm in the stillness
stirred against its hide —
a deliberate twitch
on one of its thighs I'd insist
— a voluntary tic,
on account thereafter,
an allusion of laughter,
flickered in the shroud
of its camoflauged profile.

It was there or just below,
where I'd seen the creek's current slow
to a level beneath which
the mark I'd gouged into the ever-sloughing
bank last week, even after the rains
intimated beavers had nocturnally-engineered
one muscular expletive of a log jam ...
so damn near their muddy igloo lodge,
crammed with a bulk of slop
and denuded twigs,

shotgun shells and muskrat skulls
a wildlife mortar mix

... and meanwhile, back at the farm,
the impregnated robin clears
her palate of worms with a salmonberry,
and the flipping rabbit
swaddles in the raw sienna wrap
of nursery burlap,
begins to girdle — strips the bark
at the base of the toddler,
a Gravenstein I'd just planted.
I head for the garage
where my .22 hangs on a hook
with my rain gear.

Harvesting Art

Our neighbor,
a sinewy, seventy-year-old
Dutch farmer, whose spread
on a dead-end road,
abutted the border with B.C.
collected me at seven.
Asked me if my recently,
hyper-extended meniscus
was well enough
to unload hay wagons all night
and I was pleased
to report that I'd mended
considerably, would, with my
certain greenhorn enthusiasm,
be delighted to join him
atop those wheezy
50-pound bales, six
and seven tiers deep
— under the illusion
of the enlargement …
of the pumpkin floodlight,
mid-July apricot moon.

Dear Brother

I'm driving down this hamburger
strip mall, rain on the slick
with oil of asphalt slabbing,
hemorrhoids pinched
in the cabin's cracks of torn vinyl
and the pricking of springs
at the junction of the construction
interstate bumpy bouncy detours
circumnavigating the old world
turned anew & hungry in my desperation
to reach you — stare into your deep,
dad and grandmother green eyes
deep into your Grand Canyon
psyche veiled in a morphine blanket
reach you in our fraternal meeting place

dear brother
I wish we could've said more
 — more of the right things
in those latter days after the two of us
stood together by the coffin of our father.
We couldn't believe
he could be so silent there
involuntary belches of postmortem
stomach acid the egregious mortician
failed to completely evacuate —
stains on his white collar
dress shirt selected for stiffness.
We couldn't fully believe
the old man was dead
there in the late afternoon Phoenix,
where old men go to die
with sclera-this and sarco-that,

leave their wives, our mothers
trembling after five decades
of vituperation and togetherness;
there by a purling pond,
gurgling in the maudlin foyer
offering temporary refuge
from the gut-wrenching
viewing room reality; inside speakers
purging with hisses of dust
and the everyday all-day
organ arrangements

dear brother
the funeral director fucked-up with that
Acker Belk or Pete Fountain tape —
Life obtuse, abstruse dear brother
guru shaman mystic who
read and read, fed your fucking head
'til midnight late September,
please don't die today
I'm still so many miles away
I'm driving and my neck is frozen –
driving my dear brother
driving this hamburger
chocolate milkshake slurping highway
where our old world acquiesces to the new.
I'm hungry in my desperation to reach you,

my brother, my third parent
who led me down a path of enlightenment,
schooled me in the crazy shit
I cherish today. You, who cowboyed
and sped like a sports car
speed-crazed demon thru
the Santa Cruz mountains,

lived in a chicken coop
with Neitzche and Heidegger,
Kirkegaard and Camus. Your contemporaries
were guys named Morley and Zoo.
You were an intellectual,
existential hippie who
got your masters in acid,
doctorate in peyote. a brilliant
Cherokee Jew, my brother,
pounding on one of old John's Djembe Dragons
in a cave he'd dug entirely by hand;
edified the UC Santa Cruz philosophy professors,
… I remember your reckless days,

my dear brother, rest in peace now …
rest in the dawn of your awakening
I hope to see you again in a place
where I may forgive you.

Annual Work Party

It was an annual work party wingding
that I'd been permitted to partake in,
and I was flattered so much
milk-fed ass in faded jeans
was mine for the ogling ... mind-boggling,
those farm girls, stout but seductive,
were bucking bales like men buck bales,
and magically, still held the secret charm
– an imperceptible distaff redolence,
filtering through the nostrils
to the solar plexus – the nexus,
a pastoral scent off of the summer
and tedding plains. Their sheep dogs played
smart little games all night, nosing
a child's football around and growling
as if it were otherworldly, ever-alert
to the nuances that we, the two-legged
human dogs, seemed to recognize
and applaud with utter amusement
and superiority.

The cock-eyed children were grimy
and obtuse, just like their cock-eyed,
inbred tar-heel sires, who,
threatened them all night long
with a beating of belts and wooden spoons.

A laboring man who faces physical tasks
as if they were competitions, I would not
wither or grouse
when a blood vessel broke in my foot.
I'd endure the nausea that accompanies fatigue,
work through it

with an educated stamina —
the 'second wind' one discovers
in one's passion for pain, inclusive, moreover,
to the likes of adventuring poets
and field marines.

But the ploughboys thought they'd
break the outsider …
"the dude from down the road a piece
– him, who don't know fer no heifers"
and yet, I completed my commitment
— finished what I'd begun.
I wouldn't go home broken,
as I sensed they'd erroneously foreseen.

When the last bale was bucked,
I shook some callused hands,
but refused the offerings
of foul midnight nourishments, the niggardly
unfold, billfold-fingering of cash.

I'm certain they'd never understand
why I declined the latter. They wouldn't see
my need for that night of theirs,
nor would they appreciate the aesthetics
of returning home at midnight,
smelling like a slave ship on the sea one month.

I was desperate for that evening
— those fifteen hundred bales of hay
No monies necessary
for that gloriously exhausting
— evening adventure of hay.

"... somethin' happenin' here ..."
a Northwest portrait

The Dutchman and I dug a post hole
in a field frozen stiff. His draft horses
grazed by the roadside, tore frigid tufts
of sere forage rye; three quarter tons
of thunder... of pummeling psi, it seemed
laid impressions that measured
in the near-solid sod, an epic half-foot deep.
The still pasture carried on it
— the wild, isolated gait of these two
robust studs, shod with hooves
like jack hammer jolts,
in a slop of manure and mud.

A slurry of Red Man chaw
always filled this rancher's gob,
save for when he'd retire for the night
... slept, if he could. His large wife's
snoring was lumberjack loud and was said
to have raised a roof. He'd heehaw
about that, and his border collie's appetite
for horsepucky and cow pies which,
for the most part, contributed
to the sheep herding animal's
ferocious halitosis.

But that didn't keep this horse breeder,
and busy local water witch,
from bringing the dog along with him
everywhere he'd go.

This old boy lived down the road a piece,
and would stand behind my words

as witness, for having likewise
done a double-take, before the otherworldly
observation we'd share. It was in one of those
dimly lit leas nigh the paddock
where the mares were kept from the studs
in the field, when late in the day of our first freeze,
this manifest of Mother Nature revealed
itself to us with a twitch and a quiver
… on the muscular backside of a chestnut roan,
seemed presciently synchronized with the hoots
from a common barn owl, and a rangy
old, woodland coyote's howls,
out there on the international borderline with B.C.
where blackberry scrub, a thorny-skirt-like
concertina, extended.

The collie's eyes turned a glowing red
as the cargo light died
in the back of my old friend's Ford flatbed.

Cowhide on a Poker

I comb the forest for vine maple —
necessary in the creation of my
new maul handle. The last exploded
on a burl. I'll peel away the moss and bark,
strip the ectoderm with a draw knife,
whittle and chisel-out a cold, dark,
hefted head – a twelve pound wide-open womb
of iron for eventuating cords of
comforting warmth.

In my hair, the tangled, captive broken twigs,
remnants from an after-breakfast
bushwhack romp. My jeans, cold and damp,
cling to the atrophied thighs of an old
boney fart back from a boggy jaunt
in his sylvan utopia. God, this earth
… is odd on its axis — so dark today,
twelve-twenty-one. The window sweats
to the tune of too much bone-chilling winter
as my gloves stand stiff, skewered
on a woodstove tool to dry … one says hi
with whimsy. The other offers up the vile,
vacuous, middle finger, while the remaining digits
free fall flimsy.

My beard grows to the thermal clicking
and sniggers in the drywall.
The evolution of my face,
auburn Chia Pet bristles on fast-forward, drip
a fur of frozen rust … twisting amber,
ice tube tusks — reminiscent of the photos
we'd shot in Anchorage
where I'd sold firewood for a living.

Black and gray squirrels
do their acrobatics in alder saplings —
catapult themselves from the forest
to the orchard, exhibit new energy
from the plunder and the gorge
of our entire crop of hazelnuts
and several juicy Gala chasers.
They come and go, as we go and come
— inversely avoiding
our vigilant patrols before a window
sweating to the tune of this
ostensibly indefatigable,
fondle by a drunken fire —
ruddy northwest nipples, inflexible
on the frigid breast of mother winter.

Many Were the Menace

Japanese crane flies
limped lethargic over rye
and fescue, long legged
& loping like lazy sticks–
straight pin & wiry
stuck on automatic hobble,
some of which were seen
in tandem copulating, perpetuating,
propagating a rotation of eggs
feeding the blind burrowing clowns,
Townsend moles I'd gas and drown,
beat them into the ground
with a pickax
near the fringe of the pond
and whereupon, with smoke and mirrors
hovered a cover of heavy wet fog
bobbing and swinging, the wings
of western cedar.
My antique truck worked its art
against the landscape —on its roof
perched two menacing jays
nasty Mohawk hecklers, albeit
imperviously stellar weathervanes.

Sciatica with a Chance of Nonsense

I sit on this couch. My crooked back aches
as I watch the wind in the ceiling
of a maple blaze. I watch the horse
watch the hawk devour the shrew,
who comes out of the grass to die in the rain.
Hey wind! You're no friend (even though you blow).
Who enters the rain for the shelter of the grass?
But alas, and confident of this ephemeral nature
that I, a temporal mendicant bent and suffering,
lie fetal on this, the aforementioned ... couch.
My nagging neuropathy moves me to grouse
for the flame unto my posterior,
and not to mention, I'm pissed on account
of a Seahawks' flagrant pigskin turnover.
The unenviable condition of my
radiculo-pathetic situation
looms foremost atop the segue of minds
and their meetings, an espousal, as it relates
to the state of these zebras agreeing
to the chagrin of a community glued
to their local channels eight, or
yada yada ... thirty-two, whatever the case
may be, I bring about a fumble too,
that is to say, my compromised bag
of Humboldt boo – eight grams of sticky,
stinky Jane, breaks thru and spills
whilst I am groping — (a serious gaffe
... don't laugh) I need this ... rope to blunt my pain,
and need I say continue coping.

Lovely on the Morning Breeze

How does a good god
create a cabbage moth
to dance so gracefully
on the morning breeze —
when in the season,
she expels her progeny
of masticators, maligning
my crop of crucifers
with an infestation
of vegan maggots.
All my efforts for naught
and/organics.

Castor Canadensis

Its tail I've nailed
to a breadth of a red cedar
– stiff, severed rudder, hacksawed
and weighing on my heart.
The excitement in the pandemonium
that that night held
as it sank on the still, black pond
those gentle ripples could not soothe
 my ambivalence.

Seasonal Creek

I cut the forest from the creek
for a view and a listen to the meander
and the babble from a tower
I'd erected in its midst. My son and I
spotted a mink last year... there, on that dike
where I would later, find it munching
on a frog and paying me the no never mind
of its peculiar nature; and while
a paper birch peeled and curled, blinded me
in autumn's first snow sun, I sat in the reeds
— soaked in the slush; gawking
into the near-full rotation of a spooky-head,
spotted owl — Whoooooh, clinging to an alder's arm,
likewise, mocked me with a gawk of judicious awe.
I scraped my sandpaper face, played back-up washboard
to a pileated percussionist pounding on a snag.
Our Scandinavian woodstove smoked maple up my nose,
while this seasonal creek hurled and gurgled
for eight more months.

Benzodiazepines and Chianti

How many spills will it take to get
the tankers off of the sea?
How many more months will it take to get
the Texan, 'what me worry motherfucker'
out of the Oval Office? How long will it take
for the day to come when you sit down on the crapper
to take a shit and your asshole falls out?
And when the Xmas holidays return,
it will be like: All aboard for the psychiatric ward.
Load up your padded wagons in Little Beirut;
your nervous bitches piss and moan –
your stumping fat ass control freak pandemonium
… and yet, I recreate these contentious conversations.
What a paradox to how I love thee — you
screaming in the cold rain to my torment; but time
has a way of whittling us down to blind totems
as wind and rain on wooden retinas erode.

If You Can't See

Nothing can be said of a spider web
if you can't see that TV
hacks into your head and lays
some tainted eggs in there.

If you can't see that religion
was concocted to stave off
the fears of the stark realities:
like the blues of dead winter,
the blow-your-brains-out loneliness
smeared across the January sky
— plasma-like plastered against
the ripsaw teeth and fangs
of a Cascadian sunrise.

If you can't see, agape and feigning growls
in their yawns, snow-capped titans
tectonically engineered to squeeze up
out of the womb of her mantel, spawning
the geothermal essence of the qi.

 If you can't see that meanwhile,
most of us want to realize something large
before we are a figment of the rotten fruit
in these annals of arbitrary human life on Earth.

If you can't see that as a child,
you ate boogers too. You,
up to the chimpanzee elbow
in your junior Moses nose.

If you can't see, Mr. Stein, Berg, Green,
that you need someone to criticize,
so you had better get out and socialize.

If you can't see that there's no way in hell
to pry you out of your hermit crab shell —
no rhyme nor reason to the style of your hair
— not one trace of method there.

If you can't see that you're insane
to think that you understand anything
Camus conveys in his Sisyphean myth,
existential allegory.

If you can't bloody well see
that fruit is consumed
the moment its aberrant blooms appear
out of the metropolitan phallic idolatry
— seeping the golden guilty seeds
of city sewer nightlife — paradise
of hollow progeny.

If you can't see that I waiver between
considering life absolutely sacred
and infinitely absurd.

Australia

"No worries mate, she'll be right"

— Slim Dusty

My Love and I Down Under

Jarred by jolts of passion, sans a scintilla
of resistance, our hearts swelled with con -
ductance — great gift of perfect circuitry.
My love and I from bed and broad bay window
gleaned vistas of imagination, far-flung
phantasmagorias on winter's Coral Sea
coupled above the frightening crackle
and amid the tardy timbre flashes,
spooning convulsive — yin and yang —
its silver shafts so bright
with a strobing art of solidarity,
whereby the ample kicks of juice we'd spend,
metered our passion for polarity.
The stormy, electrical awe of her gaze
fell precious, even sacred, upon me,
as our time together perpetually abated
— unraveling within this antipodean mystery.

Noosa Heads, QLD, AUS

Like a wash cycle set on infinite,
waves inflate, roll, crash, fizz.
Faded impressions on the shoreline
of the send-in, send-out sea
— as we enter the ocean
and an energy that wads us up
into a massive, elongated fist —
grips and hurls us from the curling,
swollen walls — collapses and unfurls us,
into the hush of the foamy sunlight,
where we stand and baste …
give it another go.
You're powerless in the surf,
you know.

Photo Genius

Up the path to the beach house we rent
on this unusual island of mutton birds
and giant green sea turtles. A gull we feed
tiptoes in and around a washed-up bed of kelp.
His personality is a marvel, albeit
contrived for human viewing.
We've named him "Psycho"
because he goes to such bizarre extremes
to receive a modeling fee
for his photo shoots.

Fartmaster in Sydney

"The Owl and Pussy-cat went to sea
In a beautiful pea-green boat…"
— Edward Lear

This morning I scraped old Bondi Beach
 Kneading the sands with every reach
A cluster of clam shells caught my eyes
The ruins a figment of butterflies

I twisted my skin to the Dorsal Inn
Where I belched out loud, farted a cloud
Merely sighed and scratched my chin
One bloke laughed and one bloke cried
I scratched again and again I sighed

"*Whiskey please.*" I fell to my knees
"*Your credit's no good.*" "*Is that understood?*"
I pulled out my pistol of cheese
He pulled out his pistol of wood

Crazed to beat hell, I beat on the bell
The one bloke laughed out loud
Whilst I put the squeeze on my pistol cheese
Still crying, the other bloke wept in a cloud.

"*No more,*" said he and dropped to his knee
The laughing one doubled in glee
"*If you'll cease to weep, my ars'll sleep
And you'll buy a whiskey for me.*"

My mouth bled an ooze of morning booze
That brought from my breath the stench of death
And a wisp of tennis shoes
So I left the boys of that fine bar
And stuffed my mouth with a cheese cigar.

Naked Snorkelers

"Wherever I go with this lady, I'm having a good time"
— Author on the Saipan Lady

Lizard Island awaited our arrival
via a single-engine, fixed-wing
out of Proserpine near Cairns.
High above the Coral Sea,
one of the resort employees
turned an airsick green.

We'd gotten a deal
at 800 US Dollars a day.
The only amenity not included
was the hard liquor and wines.

The main draw was the Great Barrier Reef,
diving and snorkeling — underwater exploration,
 adult nudity, and sure, most likely sex
on one of the outlying atolls with a private beach.

One of the very tanned Aussie staff
loaded-up our small skiff for the day
with an extensive picnic lunch, umbrella
and towels.

It was magnifying glass hot
motoring across the commute
from the village and moorings
to the anchorage of our quaintly-named destination,
Turtle something. And be that as it may,
we set up and shed our threads — began snorkeling
bare-asses mooning the sun.

We lost consciousness, fell into a lazy baked
quasi-reverie from the sun's proximity
and to the awe of the brilliance of corals,
brain and fans, Jesus Christ, the giant clams
— pursing lips fluorescent.

That day I played tug of war with a monitor lizard
… the prize was ownership of the towels
we'd been issued. The seagulls were skilled
in pillaging the day-trippers for their baskets
of chicken and eggs, brownies maybe, hell I don't
remember the entire fare, only the tide coming in
on our arrangement. It was total chaos…

We were just beginning to feel the burn
when we returned the dinghy and when I alerted
the attendant, a smirking bloke, we'd been attacked
by a large lizard out there on the beachhead
and he responded with something like 'no shit'
in Australian.

We spent the next six days and nights in our room
applying aloe to our backsides for the most part.
Five grand and seven thousand miles later we returned
— the two of us moulting

California

The El Cajon Baptist Temple

...where I learned to recite King James,
commit verse and hymns
to memory's spiritual asylum
every Sunday peeling strips of dried sealant
from the white latex window frame
defacing with boredom, plotting an escape
from an institutional structure
where the clapper like an uvula throbbed
in the throat of a spire
on a north end commercial lot in Sunny Slopes.

That they'd called the establishment a temple
had my dad a tad perplexed, actually found it queer
because his biological father, reared in a Jewish ghetto
sprouted-out of a tenement in the lower east side streets
of New York City, ... went to a *schul*. I guess the Jews
didn't have a monopoly on temples.

So yeah, my father found it peculiar the Baptist's
had claimed this title for their place of worship too,
said he'd thought a temple and a synagogue synonymous;
exclusive to the Jews and he scratched his hairless,
freckled scalp, mostly eschewing the spiritual himself,
no matter the version, and with an ironic eventuality,
it was that layer, that cranial tier of flesh atop his crown,
that would erupt into a malignant scape of carcinomas.
Folks were still unaware in those days that carbon emissions,
factories and automobiles, were beginning to bore holes
into the Earth's atmosphere, the ozone, as it were ...

but anyway, my parents thought it the thing to do —
boarding me on the Sunday morning school bus,
aligning me with the possibilities of a piece of the

pie in the sky … perhaps pointing me in the direction
to the great By and By or, at least, I'd glean some notion
as to those powers that be.

I'd put on my Sunday's Best and they'd seed me with a buck
just prior to my climbing those iron-grated-like-an escalator steps
and it was my responsibility to put that buck into the fucking
collection plate, but I'd invariably exit that bus at the *Temple*
and hightail it back down to the bowling alley on Fletcher Pkwy.
I'd watch the middle-aged, 4H ladies in their rodeo getups
smoke and bowl — sitting there in my Sunday school suit and my
shoes all a'shin'n, completely covered with the extra napkins
I'd requested, ere I'd consume an order of fries smothered
in bleu cheese dressing. I'd inhale the haze of tobacco
and the rolling thunder of the heavy polyester cores
dropped somewhere upon their approaches and thrumming
the glossy narrow lengthy lanes of maple and pine.
I'd wash my taters all down with the muddy, blissful flow
of a chocolate milkshake I'd added to my order from the dingy
little coffee shop inside the Parkway Bowl, and a mile or so
from oblivion.

Todos estamos cautivos en un perpetuo estado de improvisación
                                        —J. Ilarazza-Mojica
                (We're all captives in a perpetual state of improvisation)

Ma, Your Brain

Who you were so strange
would fool me sometimes lucid
... with the sick chameleon
of your love-hate heart.
You'd become so wary, you scared me
with your eerie amyloid plaques
and paranoid tangles — talking to yourself
in your sundown bedroom mirror
— thought I'd been rifling through
your diamonds and gold.
You couldn't realize at the end
I would have done anything for you,
but I could not stop your suffering,
as only God decides the end of human suffering.
That's what the spiritual governors of morphine,
who'd nursed you nineteen days in hospice told me,
while your cold feet ballooned in my warm palms.

Humane Society

How odd that we the blessed humans
play God when it comes
to putting the so-called
lesser beings down.
Had I put my thirty-eight to your temple,
or smuggled in a lethal dose
of potassium chloride,
I would've gone to prison for murder
... not mercy.
I heard the last rites
at a bedside down the hall.
It had me reeling at the nurse's station
— that they would presume
to make their uninvited rounds, perform
the laying-on of sanctimonious,
bullshit hands, whilst I
had held a hundred untold reasons,
as to why their voodoo and religiosity
were simply shams.

More on the Death of One's Mother

My wife and I are back
from a month-long stay in Phoenix.
My mother is dead.
I am stunned … and needless to say,
struggling with the typical tidal waves of emotion
following such disappearances
I try to stay busy in the garden
or plod along the wildlife trails —
the best way for me to occupy my mind
and keep me from reviving the drama
of her over-extended suffering,
witnessing her pain and the inhumane process
one has to go through because
we can't put our loved ones down
as we do our suffering, terminal pets.
Anyway, those are my thoughts
as a secular man.

You Don't Know Me

I find myself
in this spectacle of existence
believing that:
I am a wonderful man,
though, I know how I can deceive myself.
I have
spent much of my time alone with this
self in the making —
this self-awakening, yet,
oft times, endless,
day upon day monotony.
No one really knows my journey,
for *it is alone*,
whence I own the awareness
to what defines me
and it's disturbing,
when others would presume
to guess my life.

Routing Around in My Old America

I've come all this way out from San Diego
to speak to a headstone in Stanton, MO.
Explain, to my grandmother what happened
to her daughter if she don't already know
… and not to mention, perform and view some
sorry recitals near the gateway
university hideout from reality,
phony bohemian baloney district
coffee house where veterans languish
and rehearse their lies, and where we are all
obliged to dote on the crippled soldiering
minds of Missouri boys, ubiquitous
demonstrations of post toasty disorder —
providing the ideal stage for hicks who
… write poems in their pajamas — sauntering
to a stage as if art might actually
cure one probing the pockets of his old
flight jacket for a handkerchief prop;
dry eyes I saw wiped with timing and a
prowess for theatrics — a stretch
into the memory of hell, but I fucking doubt it
… because I smelled it and it stank.
And though it kept the Mid-western spinsters
who run the nurturing programs
with their social science degrees
and broken relationships, kept the bumpkins
feeling fresh and quasi hip — it really didn't
accomplish shit, although it did provide me
with an excuse to trace my one time,
Route 66 migration, back to the place
of my birth, through the Hopi, Navajo,
and Cheyenne nations, where my mom and dad
in a '48 Dodge, stopped to take a piss,

purchase a souvenir in the great mid -
century diaspora, ala the
juvenile, James Douglas Morrison's
"fragile eggshell mind." Fifty years later,
I damn-near lands in a panhandle hoosegow;
Amarillo on the windy bias.
Cowboy American lawman with a V-8,
enforcer of lawless profiling
pony tail, California license plate
beat you to death for a roach on a stretch
where a stagecoach competed
with the snorting buffalo past. Nostrils
bull-nosing southeasterly; tumbleweeds
blasting-off of the Southern Oklahoma
state line like it was the fall of 1849.

Ode to an Odist

Publishing can be a kind of trap
for the hedonism that hides away in us.
I'm learning that with a bit of disgust
for myself
As far back as I can remember
I've had an insatiable appetite
for validation.   I liken it to
The Treasure of the Sierra Madre
A little bit of gold just isn't enough
for the Dobbs in me
Of course, it doesn't help that I
have to hawk my books for reviews,
stand up and project myself on stage
with a mic and try not to tremble
feigning actions of an elevated orator —
lights ablaze and blasting me in my
already hyper-sensitive antique eyes.
Finally, I sit there amid my stack of books
and sign two copies; drink a pint of IPA
and chase it down with a shot of Dewars.

Old Man of the Park

Fountains trickle soft sounds,
muted in groves of ficus titans.
Canary butterflies lilt
in a dusty, reflective paradise
of dog park puddles
and the twisted

columns of junipers lining
the aging, carved-in-marble bards,
reflections bathed in fountains
chipped-away-at by the hordes
of field trip vandals
raging on a zoo of smells;

And there are the mimes
who mime before the part-time
taco hot dog junk food
grease trap vendors.

Tacky acrid eucalyptus seeds
pit the pavements.
Inching linear columns of ants
transmigrating the contorted
torsos of nesting schizophrenics
released in the morning

from a Fourth Ave
addiction recovery mission,
lounge the rest of the day
in beds of hibiscus geranium lantana,
near etched graffiti
recreation storage shacks
horseshoe pits, and pickle weed.

Stone stares on a museum
esplanade; statuesque
hard looks of young lovers
damn-near dogging it
engorged with tension
and rhythm. Lewd, visual —
fall off a bench & onto the grass.

Ah, to be a child again,
encore of innocence
reenacting the smile,
eyes straight and clean,
rehearsing my balance
on everything

Sweet with the sweaty aroma
of youth. Not this malodorous
scent of decadence, stench of wisdom
ancestral cesspool encrypted
in a dead devotion to the frozen poses
of disbelief; absent any hope
of thawing-out decades,
dappled with critical myth.

Peeling layer upon metaphorical layer
The skin of the onion emitting
the lachrymator teargas
into the dry socket eye
and what it is about a wading pool
that makes a small child run.
The giddy exhilaration
in the anticipation
of contact with cold water
kissed by the sun.

Pigeons on lift-off applaud.

Skirting the Barrio on a Bike

I go into a city bar
stagger out with enough gumption
to get my ass stomped
on a backstreet where a sheet
of newspaper seizes
against the harbor breeze
scrapes the base
of a lamppost where it
wraps a wily biased editorial
around a wrought iron
bench leg in a park named
for a Mexican revolutionary
— whose political activism
inspires the etched-in-concrete
cultural tapestries of graffiti
and tribal gangland art.
There in the urban
beat-down bodega sunshine —
Two hundred years of heritage
juxtaposed to a contemporaneous
enclave of bazaars, where local Latino
impresarios gather to perform
the mellifluous saga of a stoned
cockroach.

It

I brush an eyelash off of my nose.
It doesn't move. It grows there.
I see that I am scheduled for
several procedures. I have liver spots
and basal cell carcinomas.
My torso is rife with lipomas.
The world is fuzzy without my
state-of-the-art, transitional
trifocal, polarized Trivex lenses.
I search the house on end for them,
while all the time, they dangle
from my neck. I must be fitted with
elastic trousers, a brand new wardrobe
with a forgiving flair. My muscles
are soft and flaccid. Into a pre-
demented void I stare
 devoid of any care in my polka dot underwear.
I can't hear for shit. I have tits.
My long, thick locks were blond
… are silver. Their remains
lay in sparse strands atop
a precancerous scalp. My nerves are raw
and worn from shelling and gunfire.
My parent's lives have completely played-out.
I've been married to the same woman
for 46 years. We have children
with children. And now,
I ask for the gift of your charitable
ears, as I revel in a retrospect
for these ancient arms that have cradled
the still, warm-from-the-womb,
hot little helpless bodies. Those having
hastened my once weathered, chill heart melt

Then and only then, would I know that I'd
finally learned to let *it* …
be entirely about someone else.

Just Visiting

Repulsed by the pious
and their phony postcard
sunsets, by the confines
of their literature
and eternal opining,
their basic precepts
of Fundamentalism 101.
These blabbermouths
and their elaborations,
lofty interpretations
and holy tomes.
They paint the illusions,
these subtle professionals
of disguise. Masquerading
reality with a creationist
philosophy — they can be so wise,
so pompous as to propose,
surmise, in the eye
of life's enormity, refute
the notion of the unknown
with their pie-in-the-sky
theology. So, while I dabble
in my darkness … in my
scriptures of time, my conclusion
is concession… concede with a
collective sanity to the fucking
responsibility to reason.
What would that be like?
Existence is an enigma.
We are just visiting.

When Keening

When a loved-one dies, you must keep your keen
eyes poised for the bogus ghouls who descend;
passion sucked from their possession of faces
— museum posers, lugubriously
sneering, mannequinesque ... tuxedo wearing
in the Tucson sun ... sign here on the dotted
pen line mustache from the snidely whiplash
be wary of the ersatz waxen, ear to
ear politeness grin. A plot to sell you up
to the plush rot — vulgar ostentatious
box of polished bronze and cherry wood
for the good of cold eternity. And relatives,
they'll push for the quick reading of the will,
vie for that cache of encrusted jewels.
Fucking parasitic sieving sluts, pecuniary
dredgers of the moribund, usurping from
the wretched hole in your sudden reality —
one's painful moment of closure; those black
divinities they've come to glean, flaunting
a most obscene, mendacious flush of tears
before the openly bereaved.

Personality Cripple

A socially inept man sits beside
a crippled woman he'd like to engage
in conversation, worries that, alas,
she may feel exempt from his attraction
slash attention if he naturally
sits beside her in silence, unaware
that he is unable to easily
articulate in the din of these
social surroundings — a small room thick
with a kinship of grieving Jews,
all of whom, emote and gesticulate,
spew, with inherent, neurotic ease.
His palms perspire, nape tingles,
Then he partakes in, relishing amid
the relishes — mingles amid the stalks
of carrots & celery.

Adapting to the Anemic Dawn

It was raining mid-morning — Ice cubes
tinkled in a tumbler I took from a
tawdry hotel bar a month ago Tuesday
in Jalisco. An imperceptible
chip on its lip, rendered a wee, ruby –
red drop of blood, added a tinge to the
citrus blend of my too-early-bird
cocktail — a novel exercise, I began
sipping at sunrise and was utterly zonked
by noon. Entirely unfit and a mess
for any future egress or descent
from the loft of my writing room. I sat
poured into a form of paralysis
A stupefied cast in the chair at my
… desk, at which time, I became further
enamored, moreover blest for this rocky
arrangement jingling in the prism of
an ethereal pool. The mysterious extract
of *agave azul* it seemed … might well have
been amended in my barkeep's book
to a drop of blood or two
in the absence of grenadine.

Cold Night in Buena Vista Park

On a typical drive we'd taken up to Leisure World,
one of the weekly visits to Andy's mom
in Seal Beach during the twenty teens,
I looked up and saw Ole Mt. Motherfucker
euphemistically known in my era of servitude
as Old Smokey by we marines
doing time in the late nineteen sixties,
where that sheer hillside post bivouac
Camp Horno concentration camp
was used for pure torture in our terms
of voluntary imprisonment & predestined for Vietnam.
It was less than half a mile off of the interstate
and just north of the customs station
ever on alert for Mexicans
trying to cross over
into the land we stole from them

and then I went into a dream
... I'd ridden a Greyhound from San Diego
to The Ferlinghetti City, me, Corporal USMC
on liberty. Spent the night with squirrels
in the dusk of their gnawing on soft haunches
praying to acorns, grey brushy tails dangling,
intermittent spasms in sundown's dapple of pre-death day,
nuthatches turning bark for beetles
— the beaking and the trilling, shrill in the crooks
of the coastal live oak gods

I was awaiting my nun-study-of-a-nurse's return
from her overnight romp with a long-haired
red-headed fuck in the hipster tawdry kingdom
of the Haight.
In the morning I called on her via the consternation

of an inhabited sister-governess
of holy front desk ordinance
who commissioned me to nervously prop myself —
pose there in the maudlin chamber,
still and quietly trembling with the chills
of the damp night Chronicle sheets
of cartoon and obit bedding

…for me, a once vanquished, freshly home
from war, a hopeless marine corps whore
yes, returned from war to a cold,
Barbary night of broken slumber.
And when she descended from her Victorian cell block
with a mask of guarded sorrow
to inform me the engagement was off, tears tracked
the mascara of the newsprint and the late night
bowery filth on the air
and onto the disfigure of my sadness face
a dampness of an occupation's relative residual
to the jungle rot crop of an impetigo-like
herpes simplex incurable populations of papules,
infectious, crystallized coagulations
of drooling ruby pus all about my mouth and chin
an enduring gift from Ho Chi Minh.

My son would live around the corner
forty years later, scale up that stoop with me
Up to the stained glass door I'd buried my face into
— face against the cathedral pane of opaque glass
I could barely make out her descent that morning
down that stressed oak staircase from the past.

Quiet Zone

... of our elaborate plans ...
                    Jim Morrison

We traded twenty forested, nocturnal
owl-hooting, coyote mewling, ever-
green acres in exchange for the twelve
hundred square feet of sky-scraping,
psychotic self-conversational nights amid
Santa Fe Station's neon kaleidoscope of strobes
on the bacterium of benches ...
of the wool blanketed and blue tarp juicers,
covered in comics and editorials that blow in
from a park with a fountain across
an avenue by the bay.

My tree house was really a thirty foot tower,
from which I'd tied a basket containing
bottles of ale that sat cooling in our autumn creek
... with frigid leisure running beneath and where
I'd tacked hardware cloth to the marine stilts
insuring sturdy support of the structure
& for the damn beavers and their incessant
gnawing. In any case, like I said, I gave all that up
to reside in the scrape of the sky, high above
the shadow boxing miscreants and night crawlers
— somnambulant and throwing punches
at their imaginary rivals for possession
of the limited septic berths on benches,
protective shelters up on the platforms
that the railyard jockeys engineered primarily
for passengers, and where the depot's
intercom squelch of squishes, unintelligible
hisses spitting from the lofty lisp—

a thick fog of mist in the 4 a.m.
freight car chatter
of cargo... as it shifts,
and when I heard the old song play
"Is That All There Is?" My eyes,
affixed on the mourning sky,
watched my whole world go up in flames.

About the Author

Fred Rosenblum is a 75 year old man living in San Diego by himself. An avid gardener, father, and grandfather, Fred has written six collections of hybridized poetry and prose, all of which loosely render autobiographical accounts from his lifetime as a boy and a man residing, for the most part, on the West Coast of America.

Fomite

Writing a review on social media sites for readers will help the progress of independent publishing. To submit a review, go to the book page on any of the sites and follow the links for reviews. Books from independent presses rely on reader-to-reader communications.

For more information or to order any of our books, visit:
http://www.fomitepress.com/our-books.html

More poetry from Fomite...
Anna Blackmer — *Hexagrams*
L. Brown — *Loopholes*
Sue D. Burton — *Little Steel*
Christine Butterworth-McDermott — *Evelyn As*
Christine Butterworth-McDermott — *The Spellbook of Fruit and Flowers*
David Cavanagh— *Cycling in Plato's Cave*
Rajnesh Chakrapani — *The Repetition of Exceptional Weeks*
James Connolly — *Picking Up the Bodies*
Benjamin Dangl — *A World Where Many Worlds Fit*
Greg Delanty — *Behold the Garden*
Greg Delanty — *Loosestrife*
Mason Drukman — *Drawing on Life*
J. C. Ellefson — *Foreign Tales of Exemplum and Woe*
Anna Faktorovich — *Improvisational Arguments*
Peter Fortunato — *World Headquarters*
Barry Goldensohn — *Snake in the Spine, Wolf in the Heart*
Barry Goldensohn — *The Hundred Yard Dash Man*
Barry Goldensohn — *The Listener Aspires to the Condition of Music*
Barry Goldensohn — *Visitors Entrance*
Lorrie Goldensohn — *Little Fish*
R. L. Green — *When You Remember Deir Yassin*
KJ Hannah Greenberg — *Beast There—Don't That*
Kevin Hadduck — *Beloved Brother, Beloved Sister*
John Hawkins — *Mirror to Mirror*
Christopher Heffernan — *[laughter]*
Gail Holst-Warhaft — *Lucky Country*
Judith Kerman — *Definitions*
Yahia Lababidi — *Quarantine Notes*
Joseph Lamport — *Enlightenment*
Raymond Luczak — *A Babble of Objects*

Fomite

Kate Magill — *Roadworthy Creature, Roadworthy Craft*
Tony Magistrale — *Entanglements*
Gary Mesick — *General Discharge*
Giorigio Mobili — *Sunken Boulevards*
Andreas Nolte — *Mascha: The Poems of Mascha Kaléko*
Sherry Olson — *Four-Way Stop*
Brett Ortler — *Lessons of the Dead*
David Polk — *Drinking the River*
Janice Miller Potter — *Meanwell*
Janice Miller Potter — *Thoreau's Umbrella*
Philip Ramp — *Arrivals and Departures*
Philip Ramp — *The Melancholy of a Life as the Joy of Living It Slowly Chills*
Joseph D. Reich — *A Case Study of Werewolves*
Joseph D. Reich — *Connecting the Dots to Shangrila*
Joseph D. Reich — *The Derivation of Cowboys and Indians*
Joseph D. Reich — *The Hole That Runs Through Utopia*
Joseph D. Reich — *The Housing Market*
Kenneth Rosen and Richard Wilson — *Gomorrah*
Fred Rosenblum — *Of Our Elaborate Plans*
Fred Rosenblum — *Playing Chicken with an Iron Horse*
Fred Rosenblum — *Tramping Solo*
Fred Rosenblum — *Vietnumb*
David Schein — *My Murder and Other Local News*
Harold Schweizer — *Miriam's Book*
Scott T. Starbuck — *Carbonfish Blues*
Scott T. Starbuck — *Hawk on Wire*
Scott T. Starbuck — *Industrial Oz*
Seth Steinzor — *Among the Lost*
Seth Steinzor — *Once Was Lost*
Seth Steinzor — *To Join the Lost*
Susan Thomas — *In the Sadness Museum*
Susan Thomas — *Silent Acts of Public Indiscretion*
Susan Thomas — *The Empty Notebook Interrogates Itself*
Sharon Webster — *Everyone Lives Here*
Tony Whedon — *The Tres Riches Heures*
Tony Whedon — *The Falkland Quartet*
Claire Zoghb — *Dispatches from Everest*

Fomite

Dual language titles from Fomite

www.ingramcontent.com/pod-product-compliance
Lightning Source LLC
Chambersburg PA
CBHW031249120626
46545CB00007B/2722